I0485634

# Adult Coloring Book

# Cats

Relax with this Calming, Stress
Managment, Adult Coloring Book of Cats
and Kittens

Grahame David Garlick

www.southshorepublications.com

Copyright © 2015 SouthShore Publications

All rights reserved.

All design work contained within this book is completely original and created by the author. Any resemblance to other designs that existed before the publication date of this book is purely coincidental.

ISBN-13: 978-1518748738

ISBN-10: 1518748732

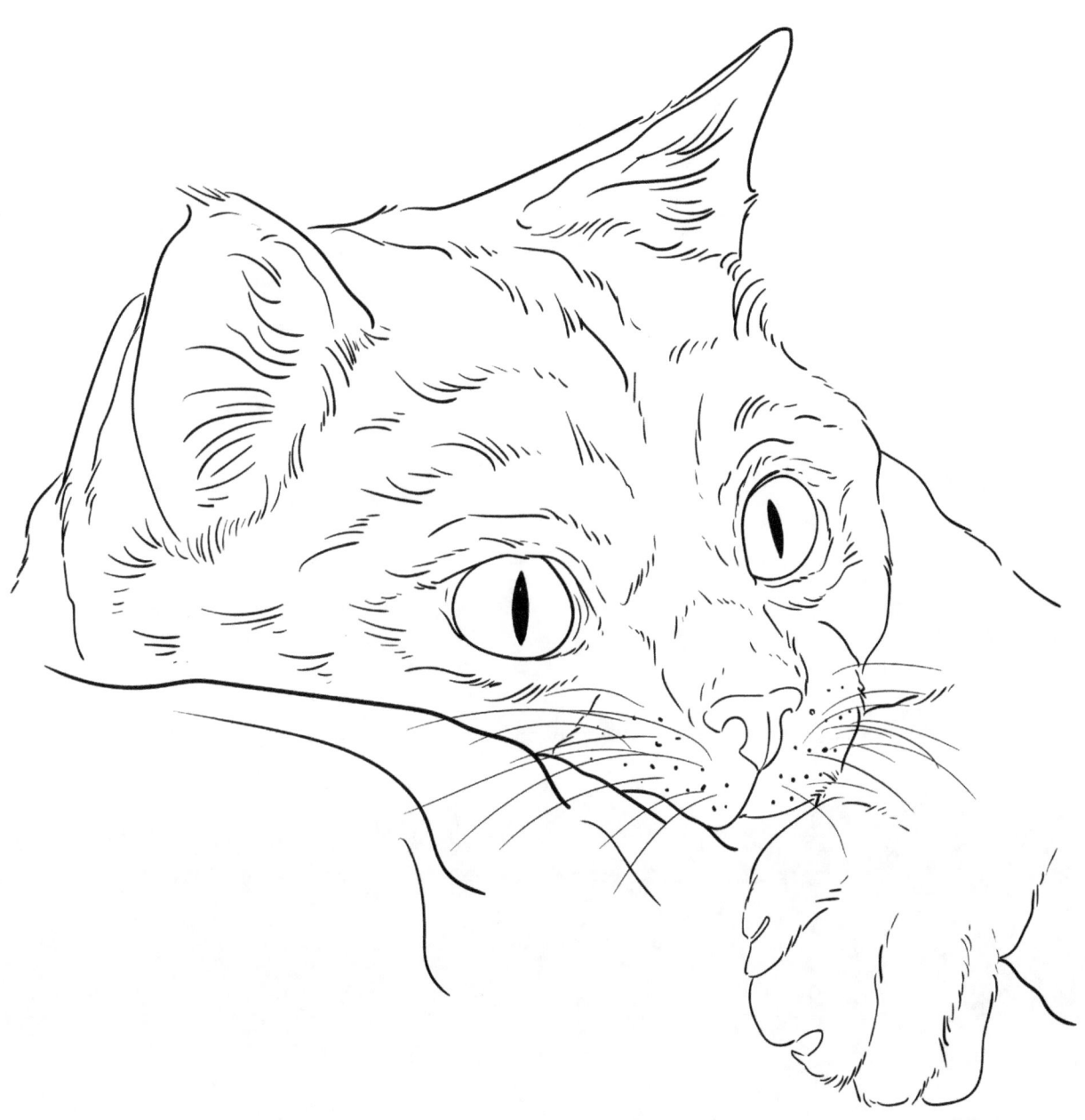

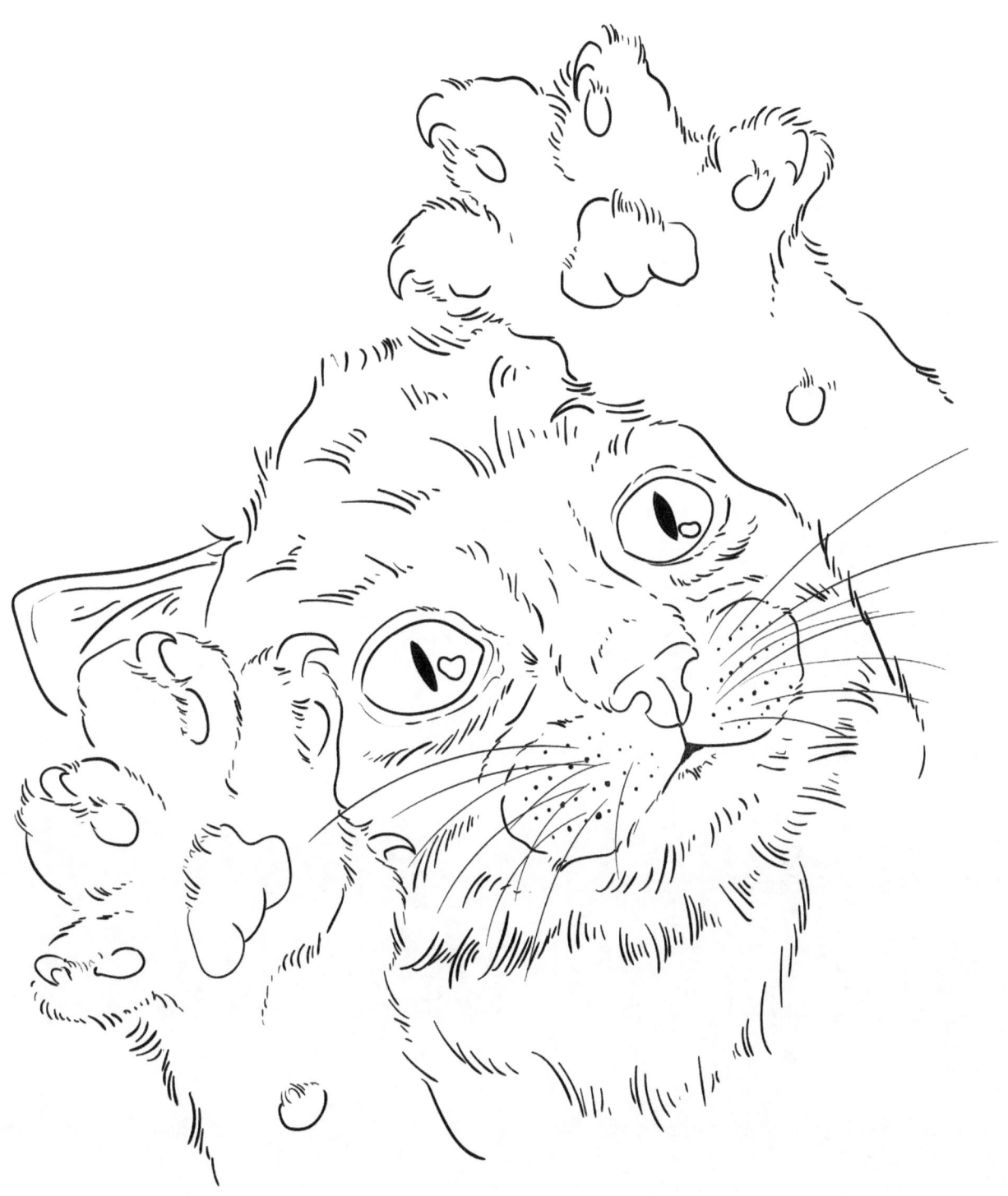

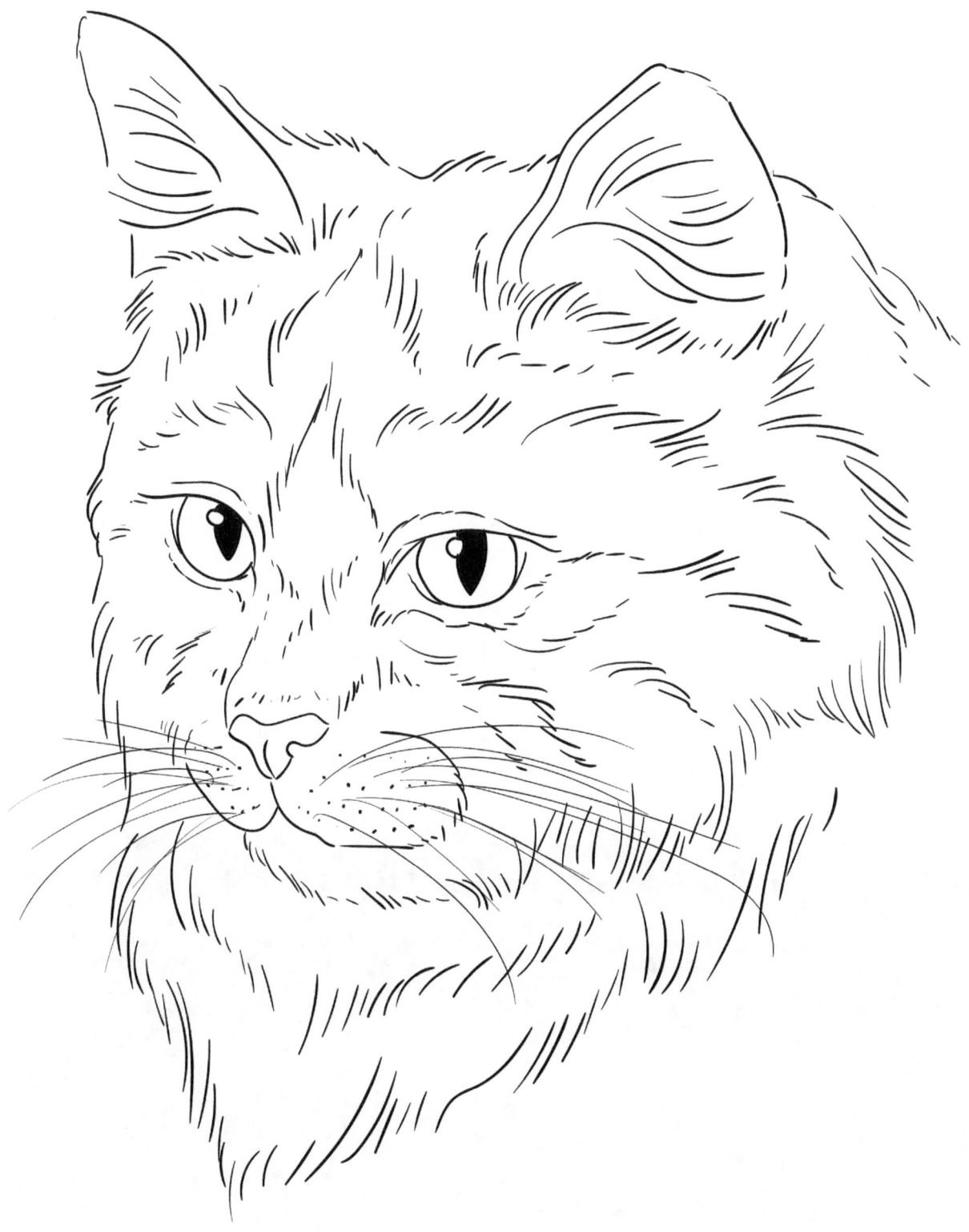

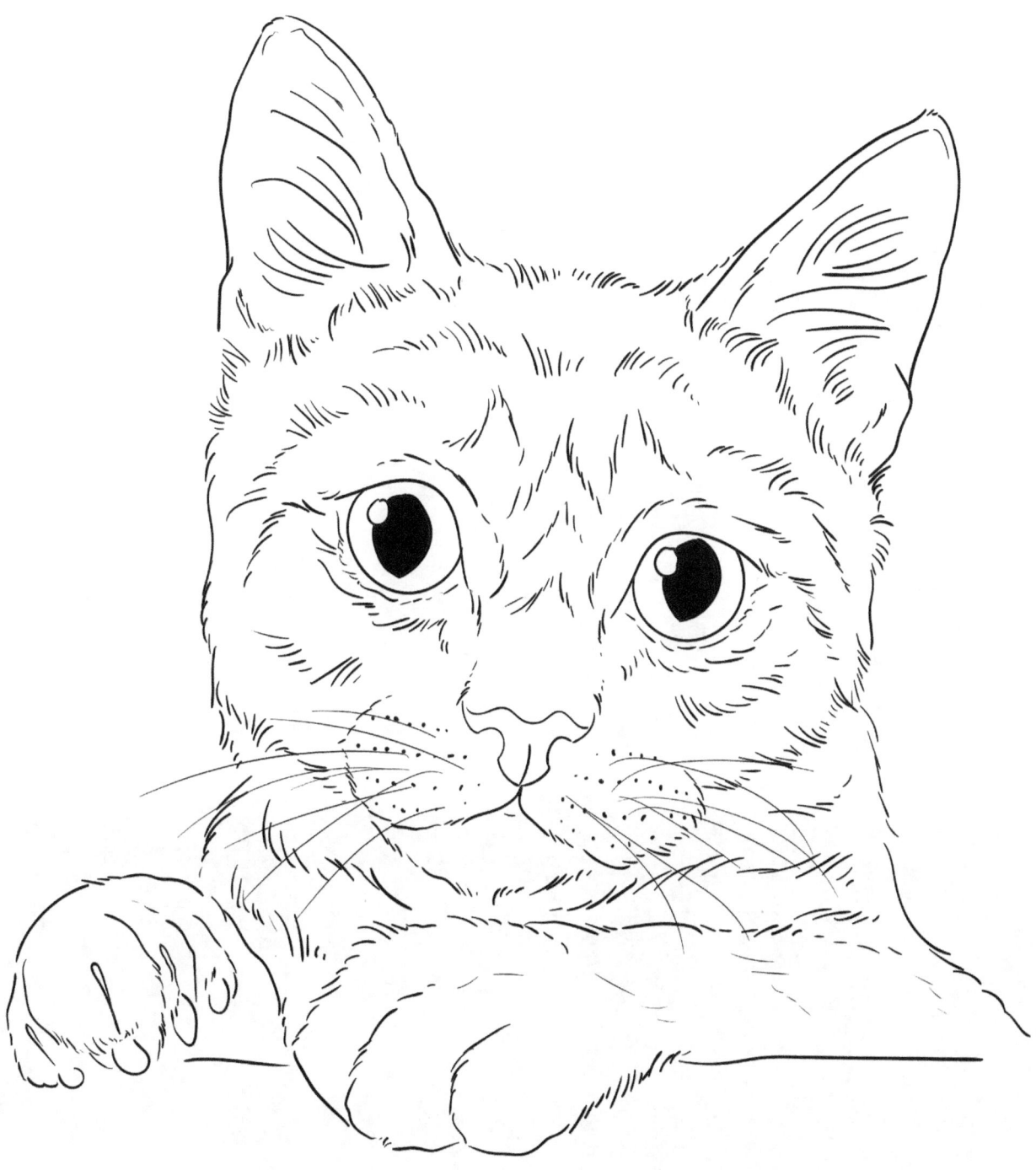

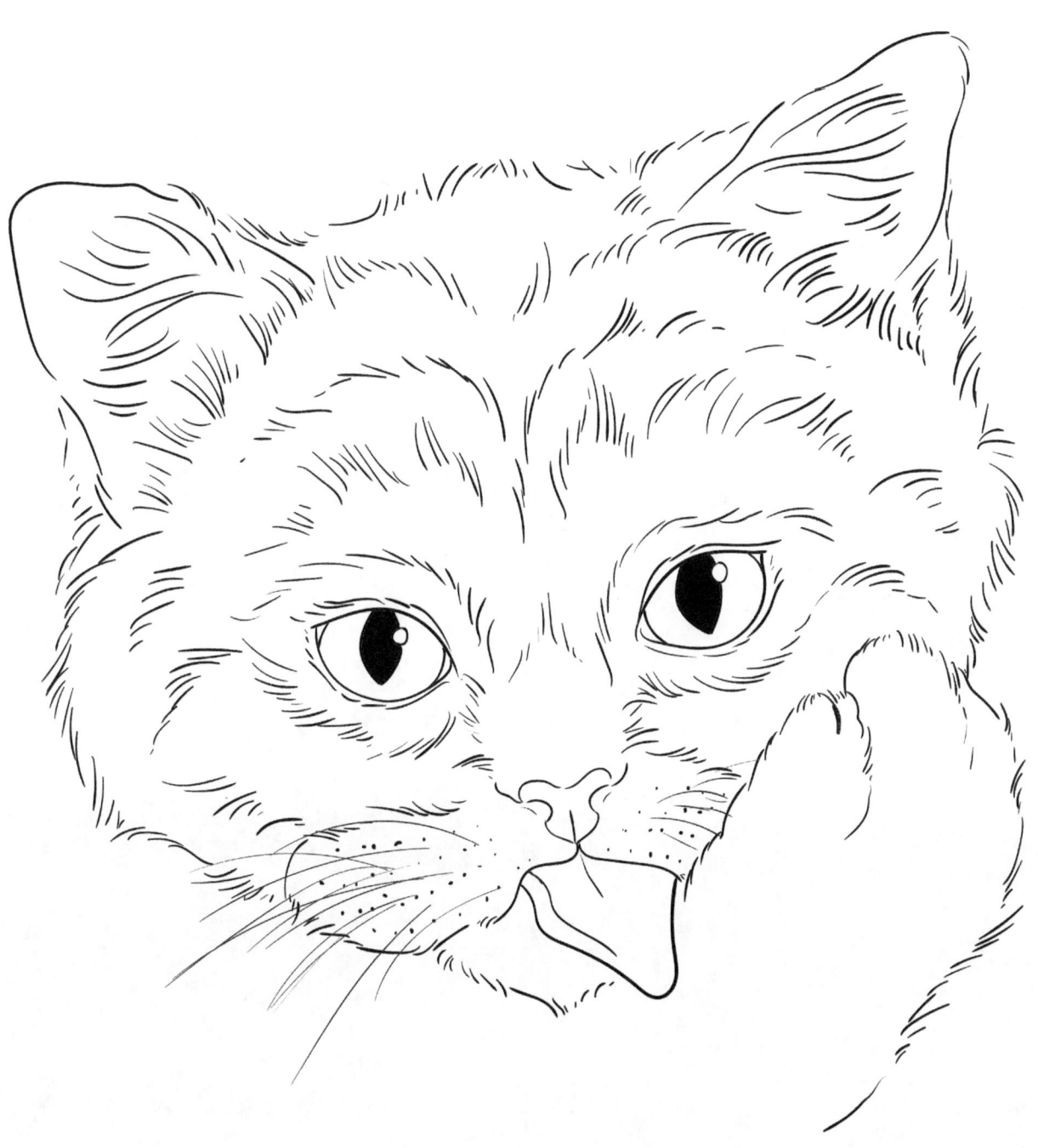

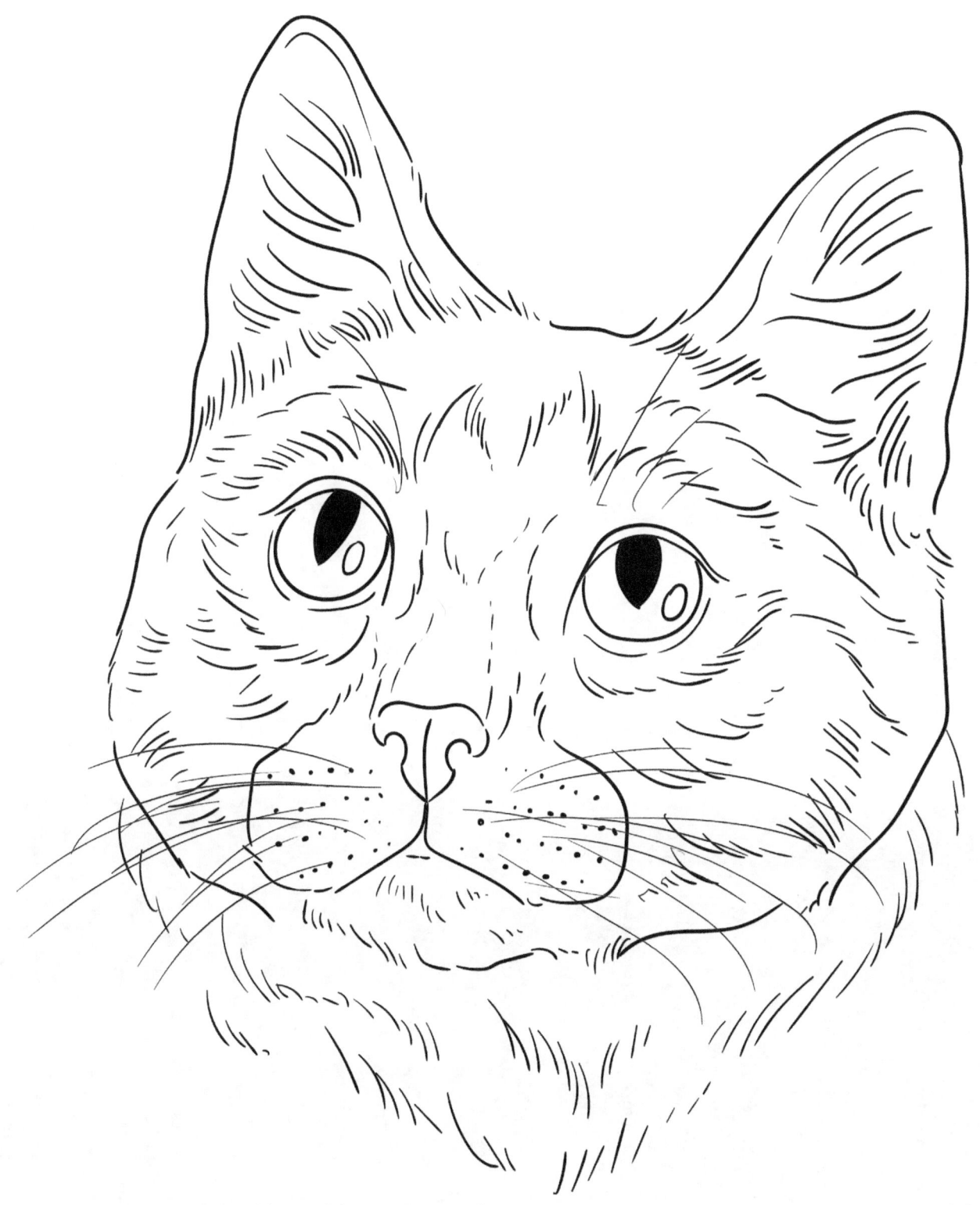

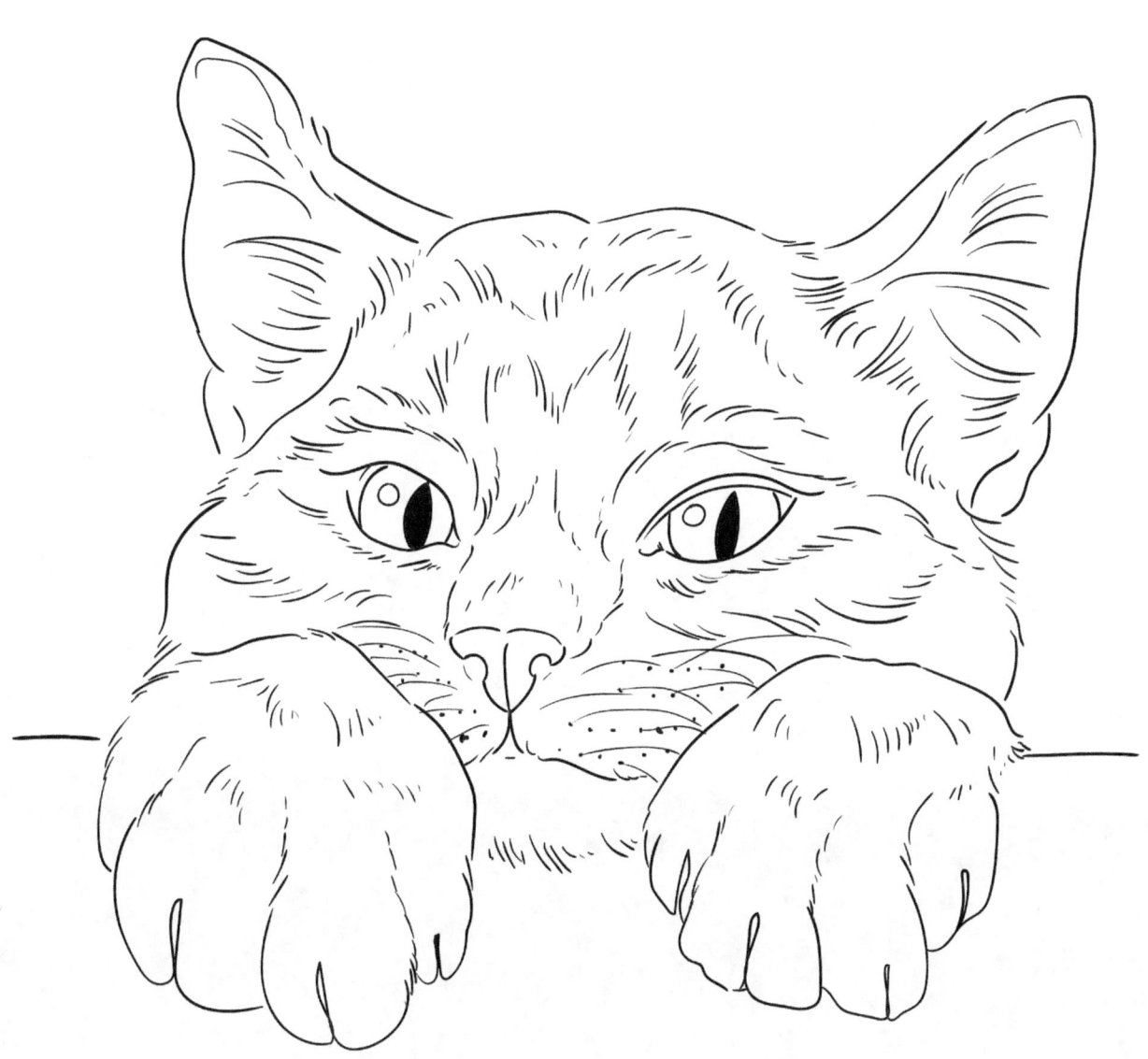

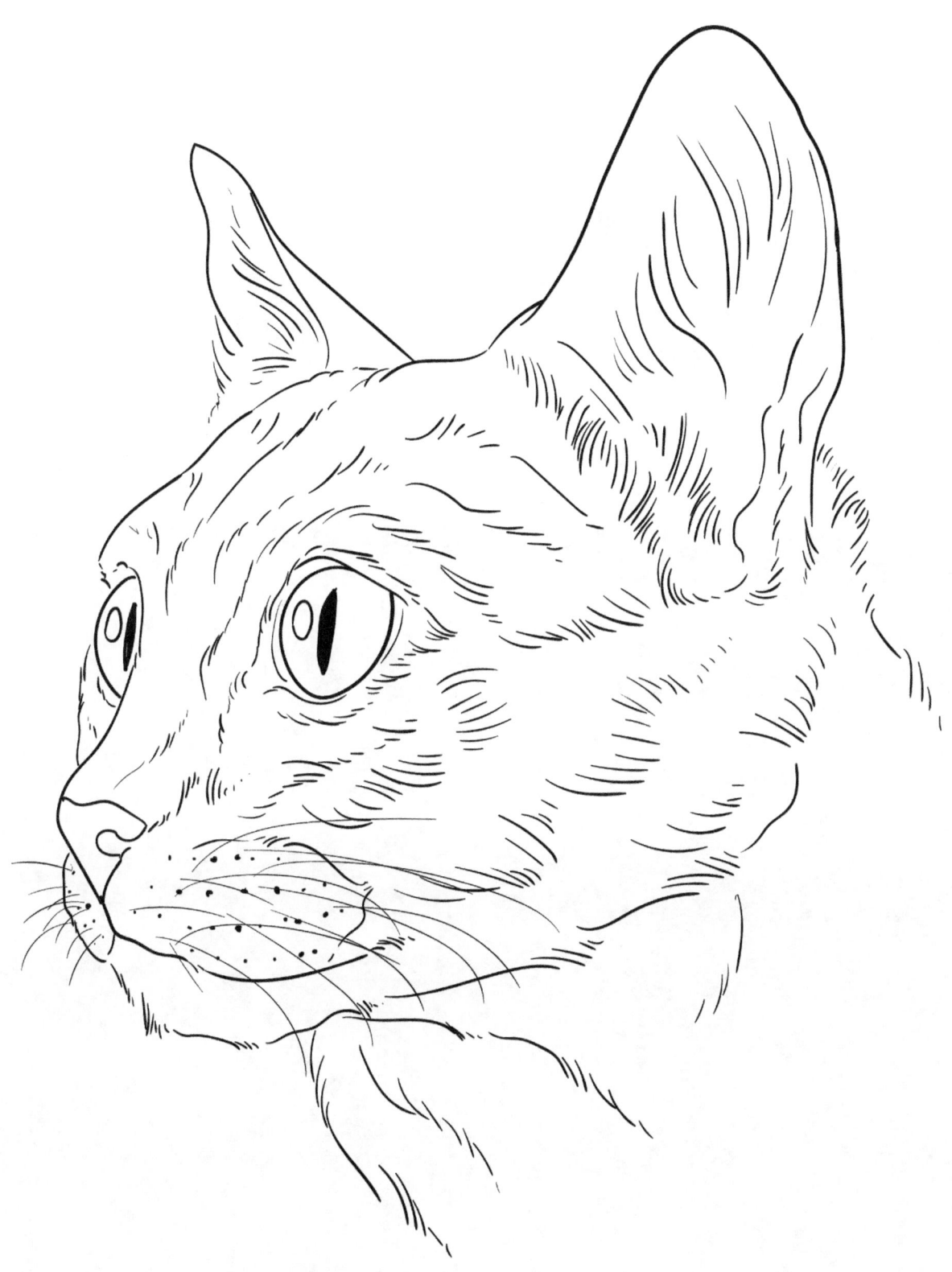

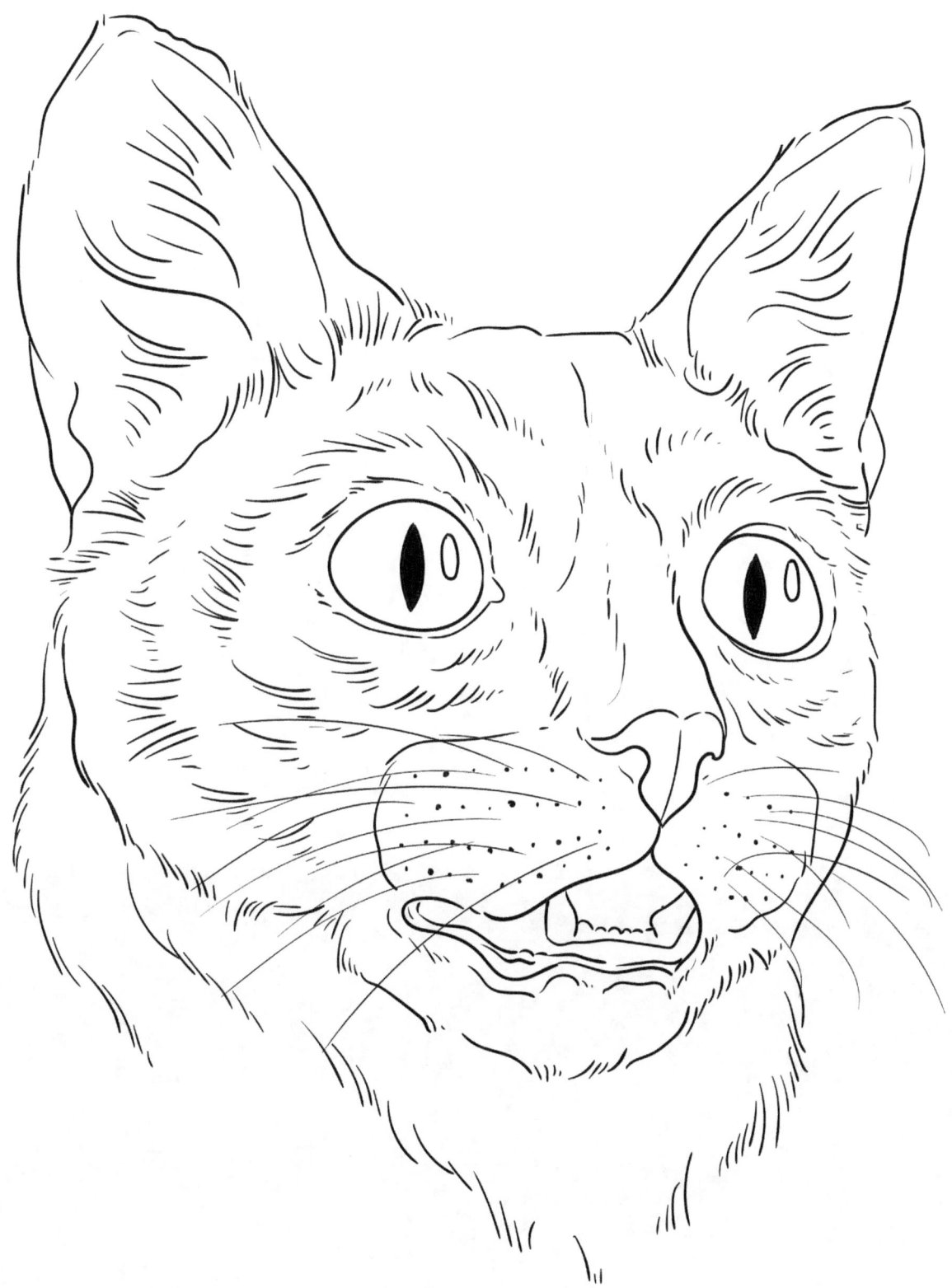

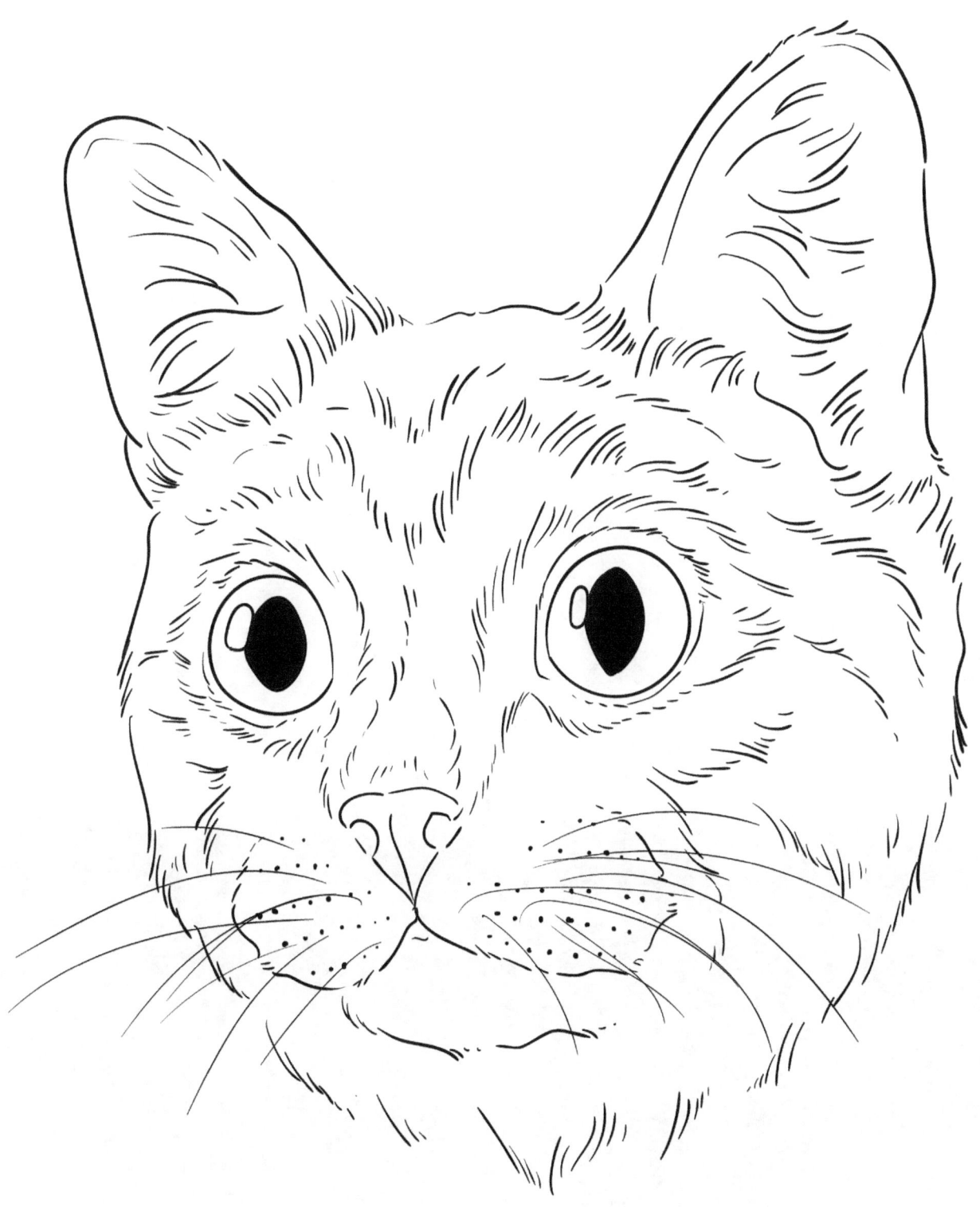

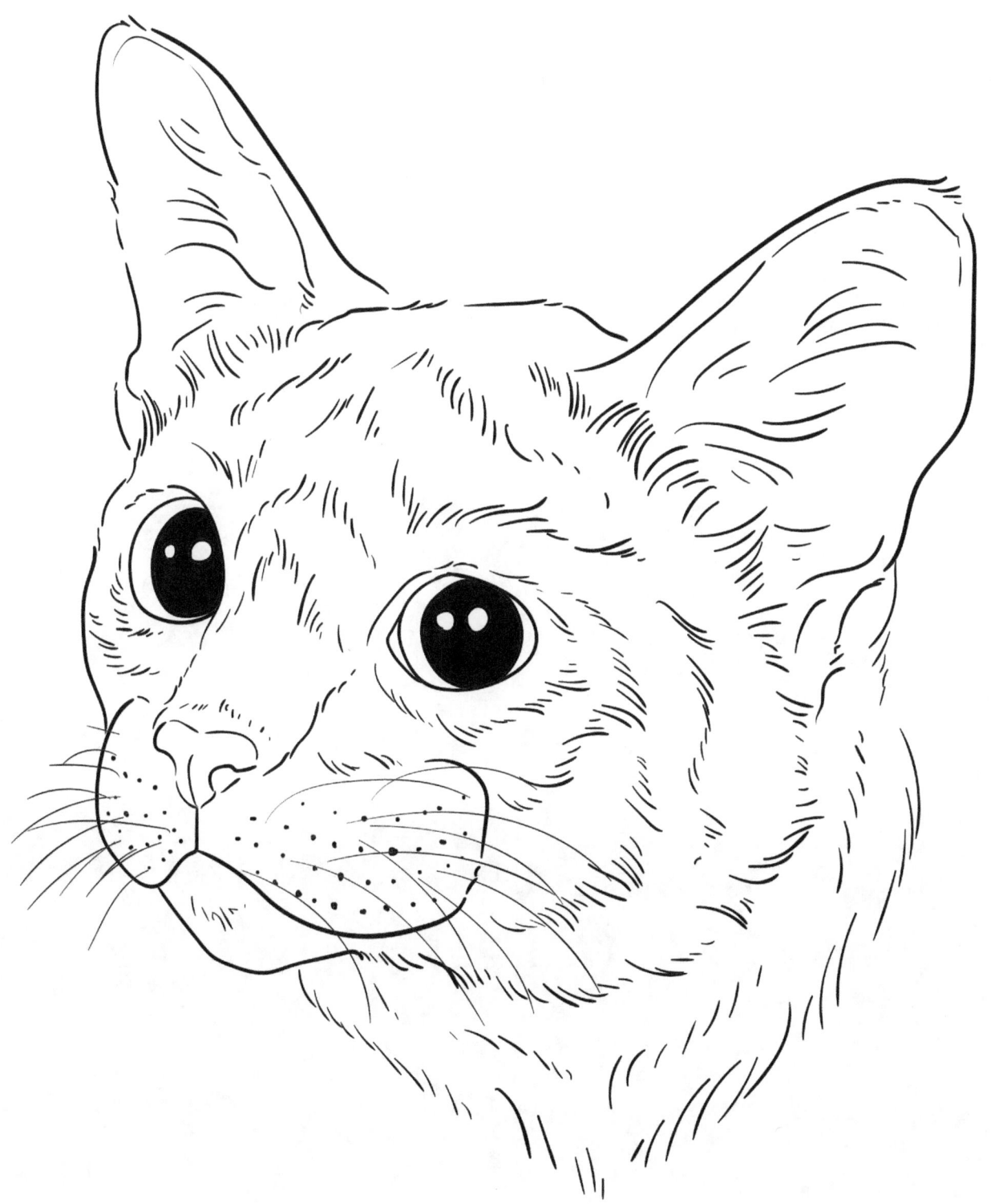

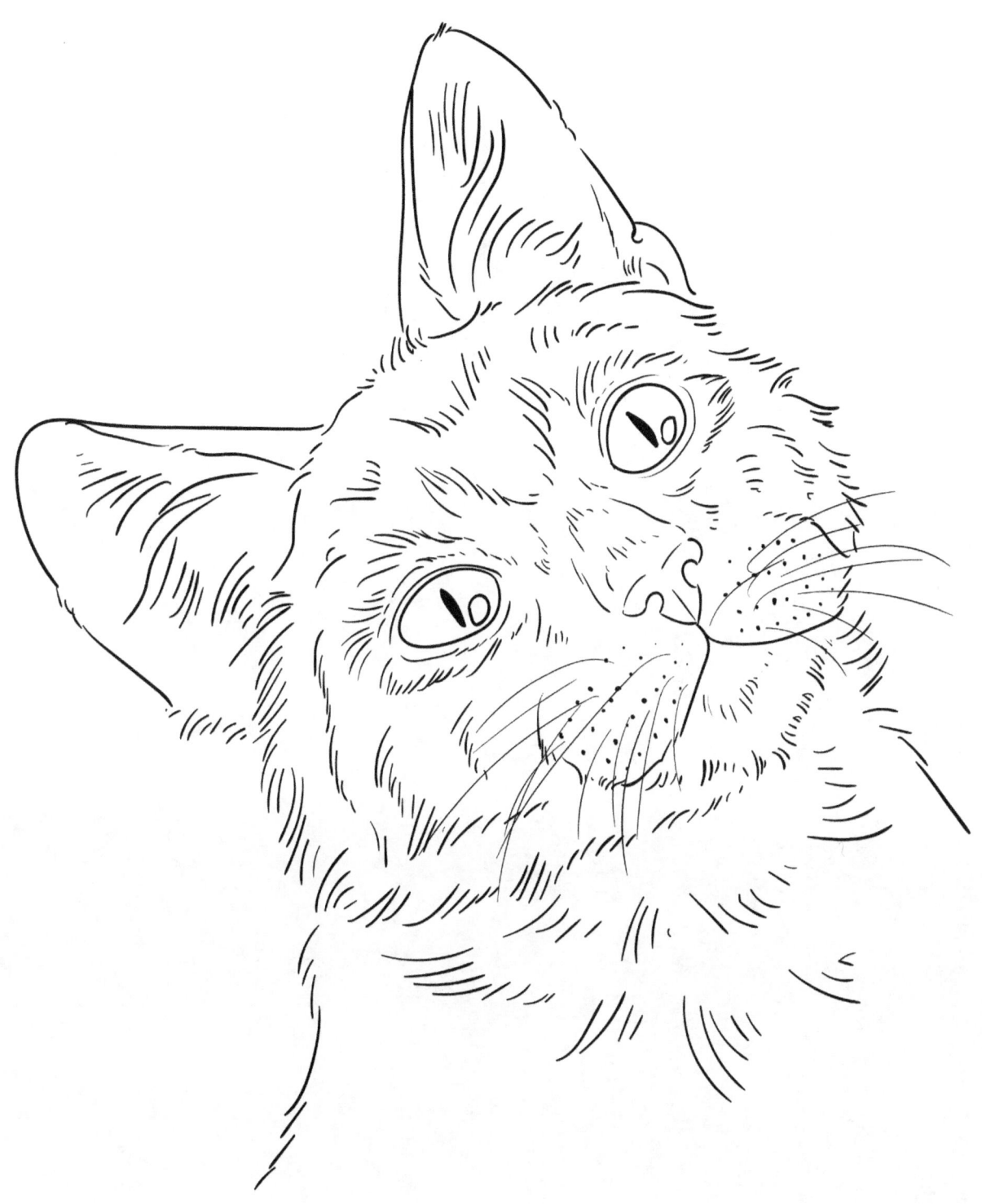

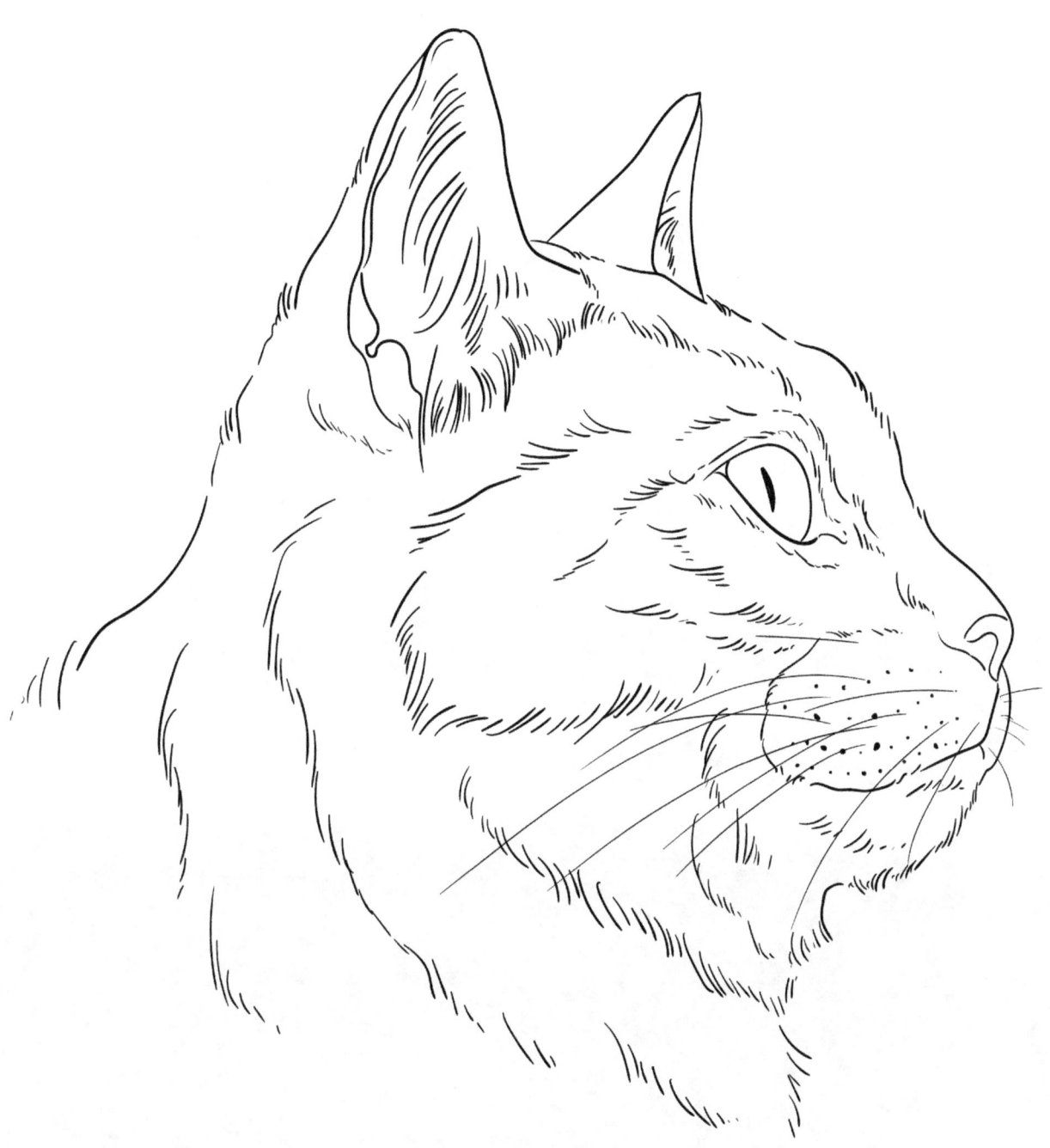

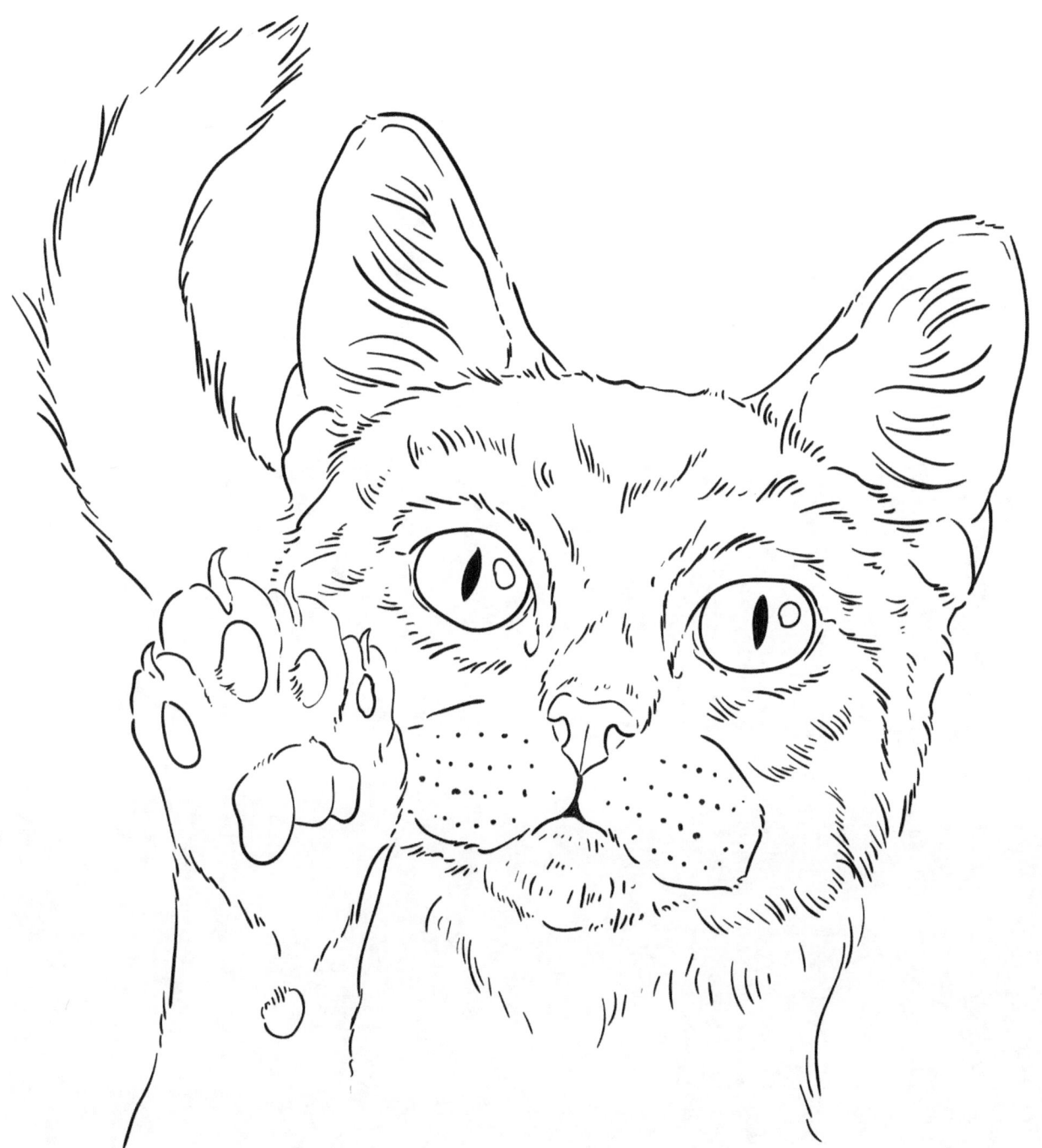

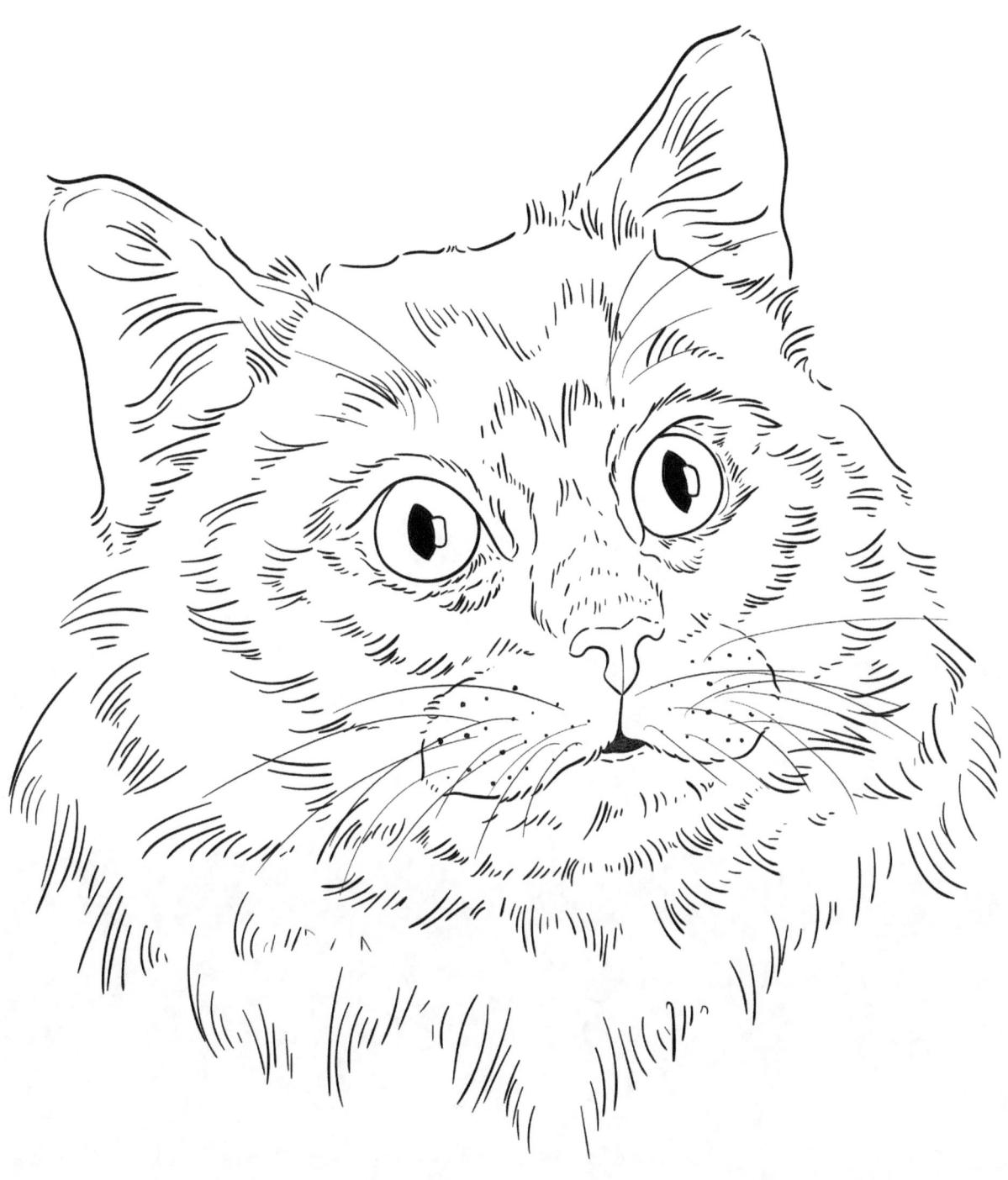

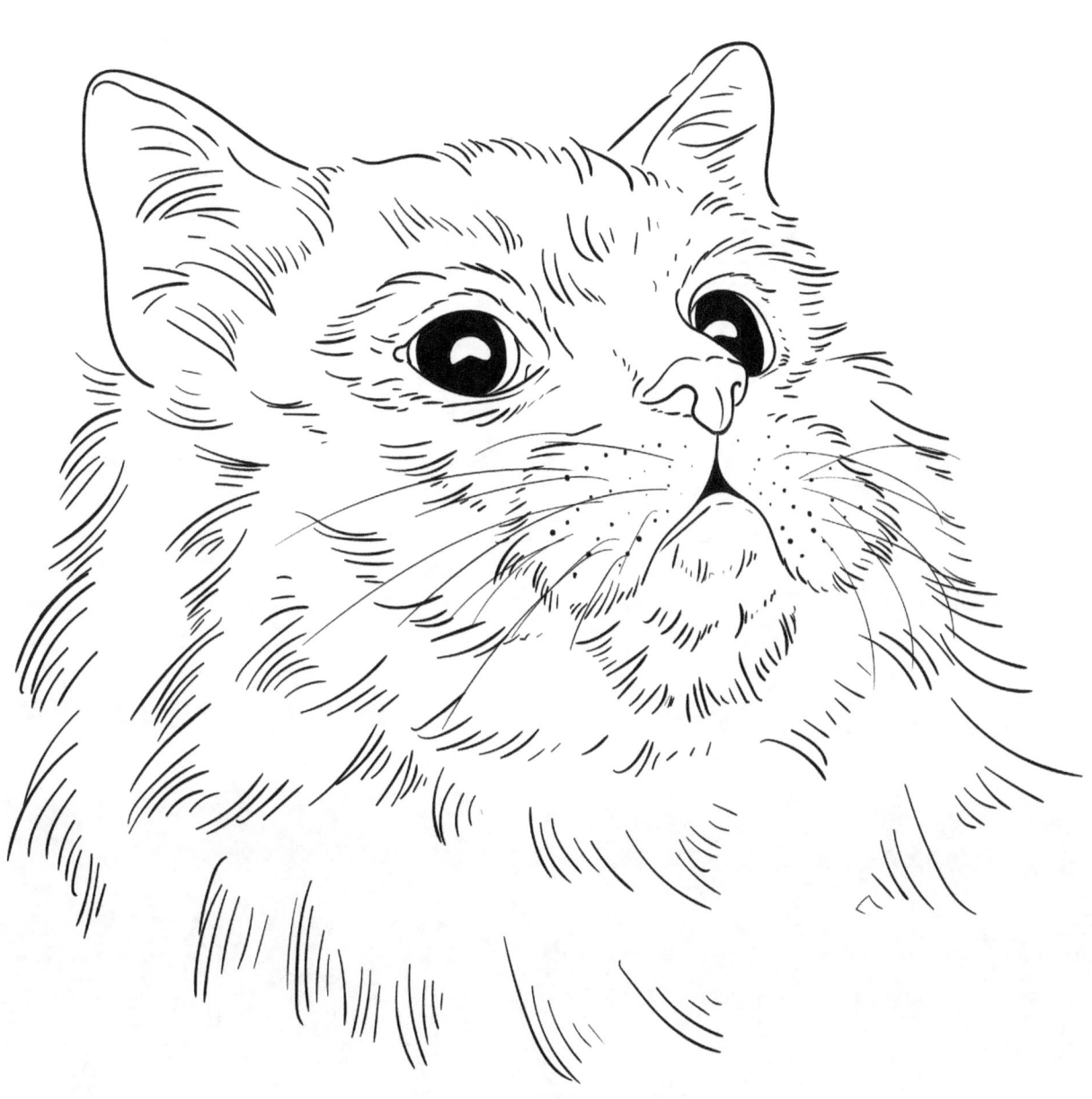

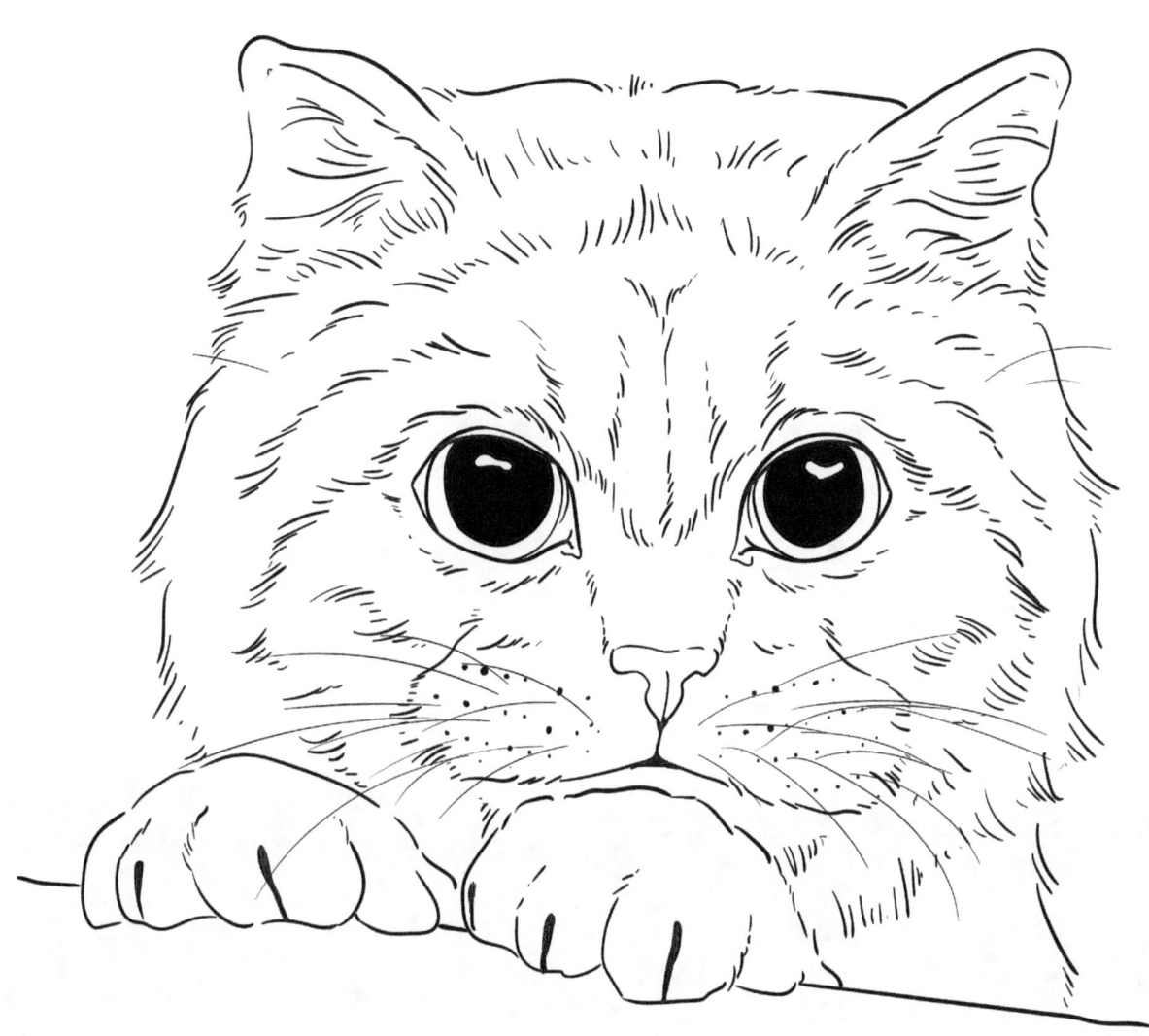

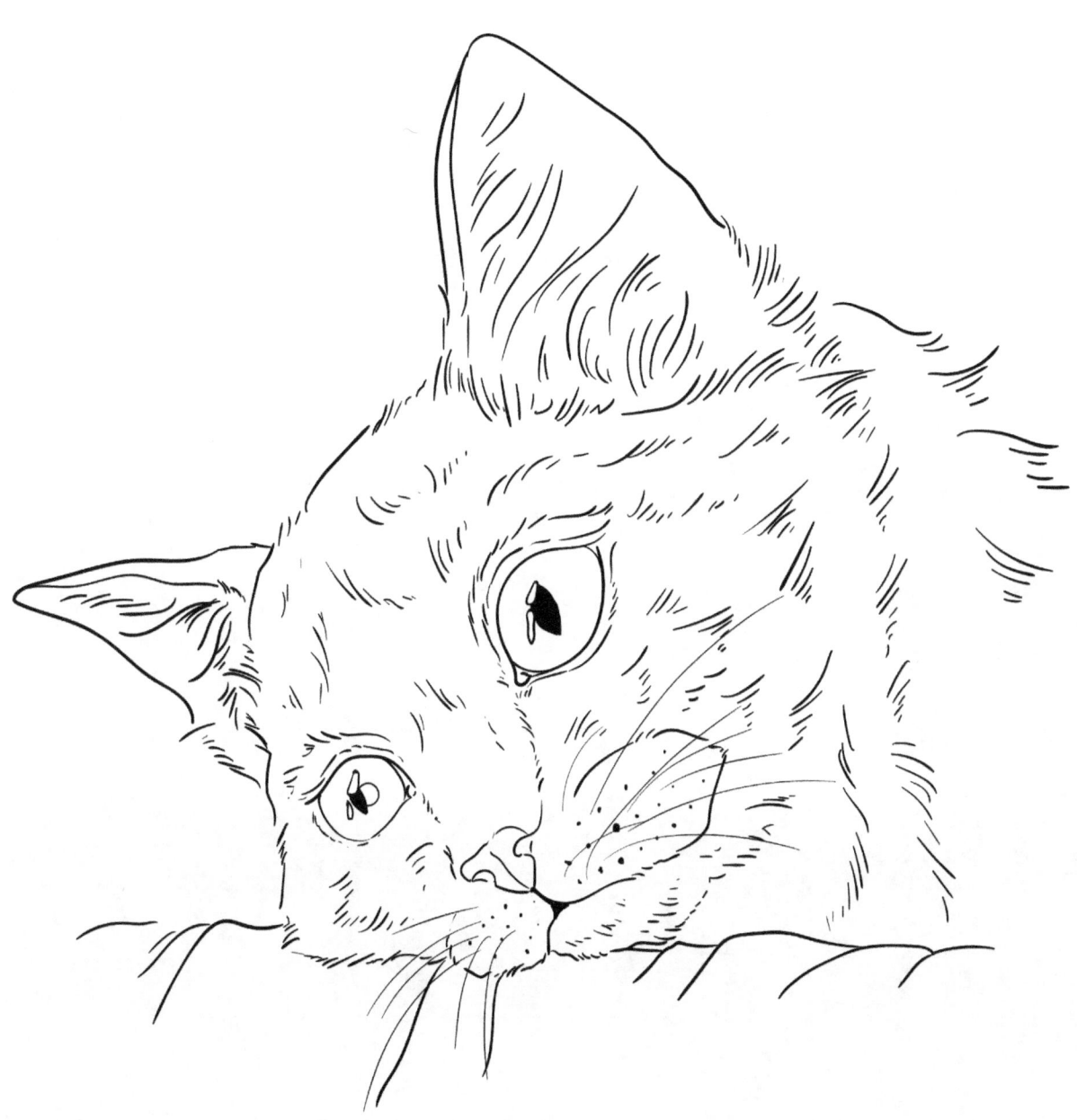

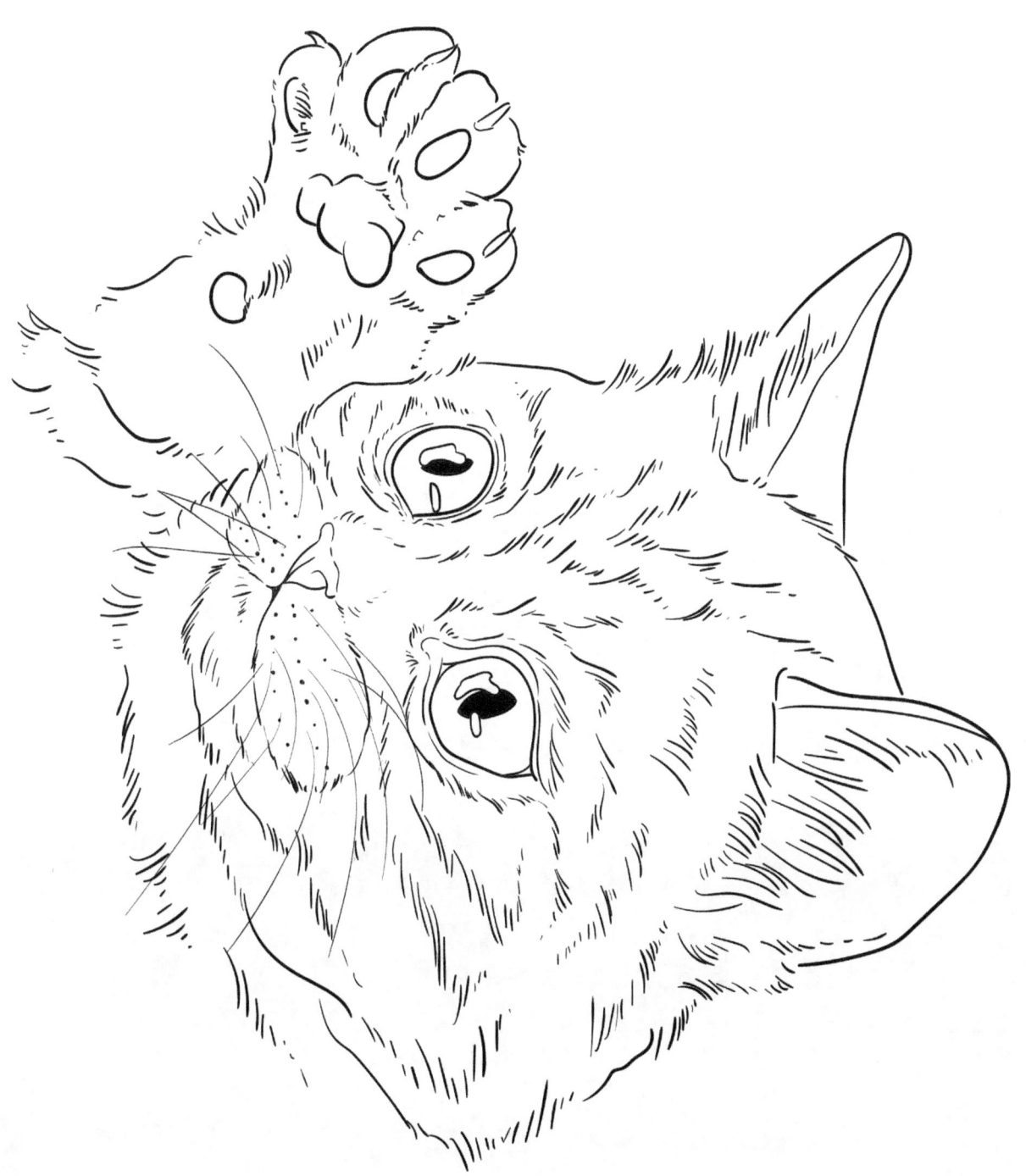

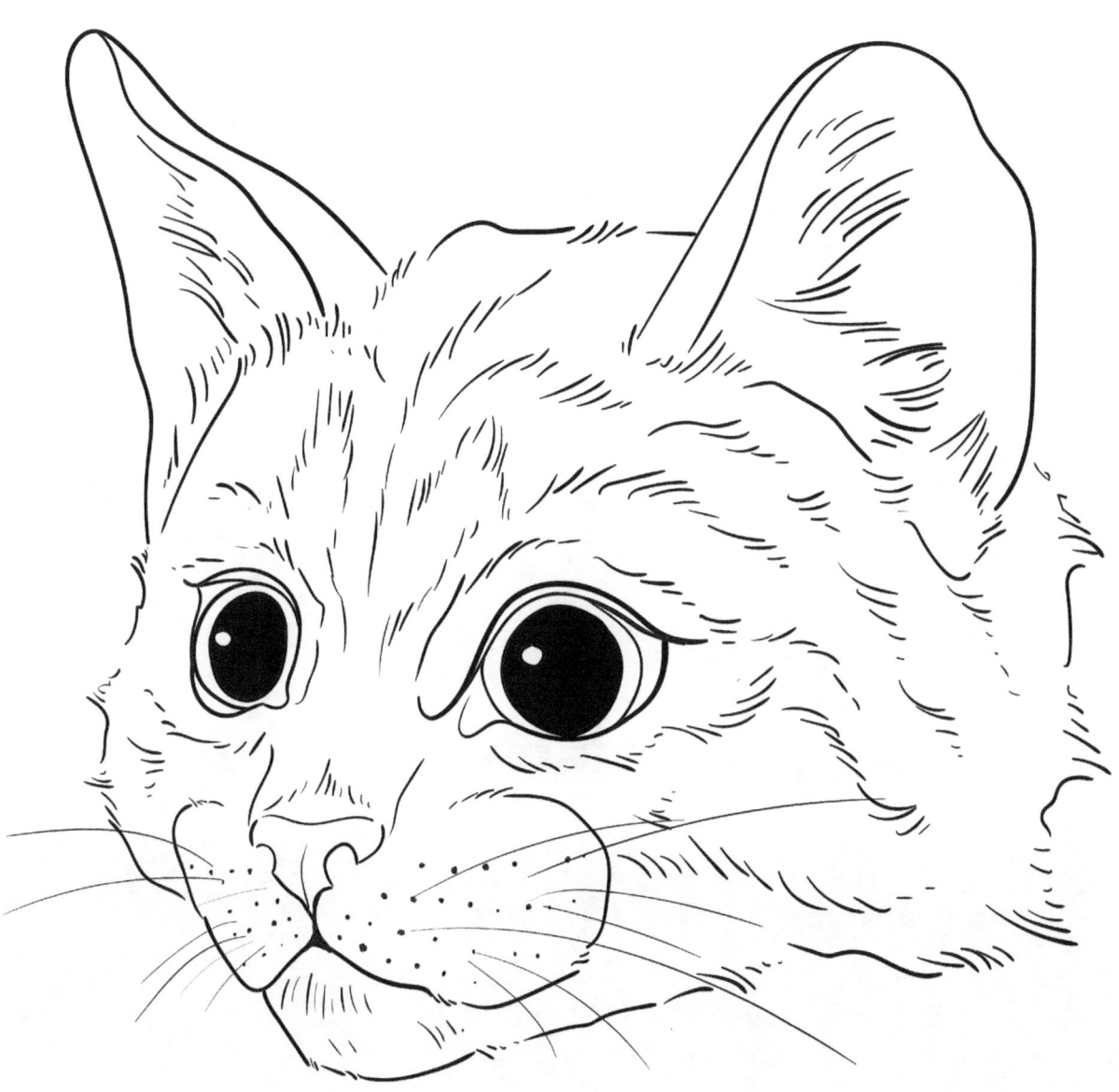

www.ingramcontent.com/pod-product-compliance
Lightning Source LLC
Chambersburg PA
CBHW080616180526
45168CB00007B/2940